Dear Parent:
Your child's love of reading starts here!

Every child learns to read in a different way and at his or her own speed. You can help your young reader improve and become more confident by encouraging his or her own interests and abilities. You can also guide your child's spiritual development by reading stories with biblical values and Bible stories, like I Can Read! books published by Zonderkidz. From books your child reads with you to the first books he or she reads alone, there are I Can Read! books for every stage c

D1521560

SHARED READING
Basic language, word repetition, illustrations, ideal for sharing with your emergent reader.

BEGINNING READING
Short sentences, familiar words, and simple concepts for children eager to read on their own.

READING WITH HELP
Engaging stories, longer sentences, and language play for developing readers.

READING ALONE
Complex plots, challenging vocabulary, and high-interest topics for the independent reader.

ADVANCED READING
Short paragraphs, chapters, and exciting themes for the perfect bridge to chapter books.

I Can Read! books have introduced children to the joy of reading since 1957. Featuring award-winning authors and illustrators and a fabulous cast of beloved characters, I Can Read! books set the standard for beginning readers.

A lifetime of discovery begins with the magical words **"I Can Read!"**

Visit www.icanread.com for information on enriching your child's reading experience.
Visit www.zonderkidz.com for more Zonderkidz I Can Read! titles.

"Be strong and brave…. The Lord your God will
go with you. He will never leave you.
He'll never desert you."
—*Deuteronomy 31:6*

To Rebeka, our grand little princess.
~M.H.

The Princess Twins and the Kitty
Text copyright © 2009 by Mona Hodgson
Illustrations copyright © 2009 by Meredith Johnson

Requests for information should be addressed to:
Zonderkidz, Grand Rapids, Michigan 49530

Library of Congress Cataloging-in-Publication Data

Hodgson, Mona Gansberg, 1954-
        The princess twins and the kitty / story by Mona Hodgson.
            p. cm. -- (I can read! Level 1)
        ISBN 978-0-310-71611-2 (softcover)
        [1. Princesses--Fiction. 2. Christian life--Fiction.] I. Title.
    PZ7.H6649Ps 2009
    [E]--dc22
    {B}   2008037314

All Scripture quotations, unless otherwise indicated, are taken from the *Holy Bible*, New International
Reader's Version®. Copyright © 1995, 1996, 1998 by International Bible Society. Used by permission of
Zondervan. All rights reserved.

All rights reserved. No part of this publication may be reproduced, stored in a retrieval system, or
transmitted in any form or by any means—electronic, mechanical, photocopy, recording, or any other—
except for brief quotations in printed reviews, without the prior
permission of the publisher.

Zonderkidz is a trademark of Zondervan.

Art Direction & Design: Jody Langley

Printed in China

09 10 11 12 · 4 3 2 1

I Can Read!™

BEGINNING
READING
1

The Princess Twins and the Kitty

story by Mona Hodgson

pictures by Meredith Johnson

Princess Abby and her sister Emma
sipped tea in the garden.

Tickle. Tickle.

Something tickled Abby's leg.

Abby giggled and she wiggled.

Tickle. Tickle.

Abby looked under the table.

Kitty purred.

"It's not play time,"

Emma told Kitty.

Tickle. Tickle.

"Shoo." Abby clapped her hands.

Kitty ran out of the garden.

Abby and Emma finished their tea.

Now it was play time.

"Kitty," Princess Abby called.

"Kitty," called Princess Emma.

Kitty didn't come.

"Maybe Kitty climbed the tower,"
said Abby.

The princesses looked in the tower,
but they didn't find Kitty.

Abby opened the castle door.

"Kitty," she called.

Abby looked in Kitty's bed,

but she didn't find Kitty.

"Kitty," Princess Emma called.

Emma looked in her bedroom,
but she didn't find Kitty.

"Kitty," Princess Abby called.

She looked in the library,

but she didn't find Kitty.

Emma stopped at a closed door.

"What if Kitty is in the basement?"
she asked.

"Kitty," Abby called.

"Meow. Meow," said Kitty.

Princess Abby and Princess Emma

looked into the basement.

"Here Kitty, Kitty," they called.

Kitty didn't come.

"Meow. Meow," said Kitty.

"Kitty needs us," said Abby.

"I'm not going down there,"
Emma said.

Abby was afraid of the dark.

Abby had to be very brave.

"Jesus, help me be brave,"

prayed Abby.

Abby took a candle.

She tiptoed down the stairs.

Abby's knees shook.

"Jesus is with me," said Abby.

"Meow. Meow," said Kitty.

Abby found Kitty stuck in a box.

Tickle. Tickle.

Abby tickled Kitty's chin.

"Thank you, Jesus," prayed Abby,

"for making me brave."

Abby carried Kitty upstairs.

Kitty purred and wiggled.

Now it really was play time.